the
essence
of
style

the essence of ENGLISH COUNTRY

CAROLINE SEEBOHM AND
CHRISTOPHER SIMON SYKES

THAMES AND HUDSON

First published in Great Britain in 1995 by Thames and Hudson Ltd, London by arrangement with Clarkson N. Potter, Inc./Publishers, 201 East 50th Street, New York, NY 10022.

British Library Cataloging-in-Publication Data

A catalogue record for this book is available from the British Library.

ISBN 0-500-27856-3

Printed and bound in China

CONTENTS

INTRODUCTION

Ask a child to draw a house, and what do we see? A box with a hipped roof, chimney, symmetrical doors and windows, and maybe a path with flowers and a surrounding fence. This picture is an almost exact prototype of the English country house. In its developed form—a freestanding house with classical proportions set in a country landscape—it expresses our most fundamental ideas of home.

This image should not be confused with the great English stately homes—Blenheim, Wilton, Knole, Longleat—which continue to summon up visions of splendor in the tourist's mind. These grand buildings are no more houses in the domestic sense of the word than is the White House in Washington. They are museums, amusement parks, obsolete political symbols, monuments to the past. Though filled with treasures acquired during Britain's long imperial history, their gift to the present is only nostalgia, a whiff of champagne-laden dust.

But the observant traveler along the country roads of

7

England cannot fail to observe indications of the existence of a number of splendid houses without National Trust signs. A fine pair of gates here, a handsome park there, a long, low wall—these are clues that, if pursued, reveal a different view of English country house life. Smaller, perhaps, and more practical than the ornate mansions dedicated to personal glory, these houses are as exquisite in design and location as any to be found in the guidebooks. It is to these houses that we hope to divert the attention until now devoted to their richer and more public cousins.

The houses celebrated in English Country *belong to the land in the way that English houses have always belonged to the land, with horses, dogs, cows, sheep, and hens as essential accessories to the landscape. They have been handed down in many cases through generations of the same family, and their interiors demonstrate the kind of warmth and mellowness that springs from generational care.*

"The house stamps its own character on all ways of living: I am ruled by a continuity that I cannot see," wrote Elizabeth Bowen about her beloved Bowen's Court. Built

occasionally in hopes of royal favors or for public approba-
tion, but always for personal satisfaction, such houses are
today sometimes working farms, sometimes the focal point
of a village, sometimes the last remnant of a feudal society.
But in all cases they have a beauty and timelessness that
have come to represent an ideal to architects and designers
all over the world.

We want to take the reader through those discreet gates
and into those graceful parks, behind the protective walls
of those manors, rectories, and farmhouses. Of the houses
whose interiors are represented here, none is a National
Trust property; all are privately owned. Only three—Dod-
dington Hall, Deene Park, and Sledmere House—are open
to the public. The rest are private, secluded from the curi-
ous outsider, little pockets of civilization in an increasingly
wild world—living examples of the English country ideal.

PRECEDING SPREAD: *The piano in the entrance hall of this home*
dating from the 1400s was produced by the same 18th-century
craftsman who worked for J. C. Bach.

LOOKING OUTSIDE

WHEN William the Conqueror, with the help of his Norman armies, acquired England in 1066, he brought with him certain innovations. One was that from then on, all land belonged to the king—the first act of nationalization in England's history. The individual simply had rights to land, rights that were passed on to heirs. The law of primogeniture, whereby the firstborn son automatically inherits his father's title and property, was another innovation introduced to the English by the Normans.

Over time, the feudal lords acquired ownership of the land as gifts from the king, and these acres were defined into sizable "manors" or estates. Owing to restrictive inheritance taxes imposed in recent years by Labor governments, many of the huge holdings have been gradually whittled down. Many landowners today, struggling to afford the enormous death duties and the resident staff required to keep up their estates, open their houses to the public.

But while the bigger houses, built over the centuries to announce to the world a man's wealth and position in society, have now become living museums, the smaller ones, serving a much more modest function, remain purely private places. Many remained committed to the working of the land. Others were built as private retreats, places to hide in after a busy season in London. Hunting lodges, which date from the 16th century, filled a need for sportsmen who wanted a simple country camp, and "follies," or eye-catchers, became chic by the end of the 18th century for sport of all kinds. Those that remain continue to exert their charms over today's urban escapists.

All these houses have gardens. Some date back to Tudor times; others show the influence of the 18th-century landscape movement. Whether neatly planted like a French potager or overblown in a Gertrude Jekyll–like border, the English garden remains the greatest pride and pleasure of English country life.

PRECEDING SPREAD: *The back garden of this working farm in Devon nestles under the steep slopes of the Dart Valley.*

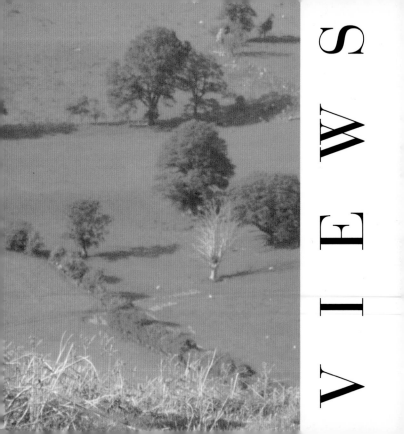

VIEWS

ABOVE: *A riot of bluebells and apple blossoms in a Norfolk wood, typical harbingers of an English country spring.* **PRECEDING PAGES:** *A view overlooking Herefordshire and the Welsh Marshes.*

BELOW: *A Herefordshire landscape gains power from its ancient trees, here in a dancing meadow of Queen Anne's lace.*

ABOVE, ABOVE RIGHT, AND RIGHT:
A gnarled old tree, a long, mysterious lane, and a 14th-century church speak of England's varied history. **FAR RIGHT:**
Rich farmland surrounds Sledmere House, in Yorkshire, where the Sykes family has lived since the middle of the 18th century.

Cows graze in the golden autumn landscape of Yorkshire, one of England's northernmost counties, where once peasants worked the soil in feudal loyalty to their manorial lord.

Most of England's farm and grazing land is defined by simple wooden gates and fences, the designs of which date back to medieval times.

The patchwork effect of the hedgerows is the result of the 18th- and 19th-century Enclosure Acts, which divided land into parcels.

The countryside in North-
amptonshire was called by
Sir George Sitwell "the heart
of England."

ABOVE LEFT AND ABOVE: *Cricket, one of England's traditional sports, is considered by aficionados to outrank baseball.* **LEFT:** *Delighting in dinners of grouse, pheasant, and partridge, the English enthusiastically shoot game in the autumn.* **FAR LEFT:** *A country pursuit: guns in position at a shoot in Yorkshire.*

ABOVE AND RIGHT: *"The English country gentleman galloping after a fox—the unspeakable in full pursuit of the uneatable,"* wrote Oscar Wilde. Yet despite animal rightists' vociferous opposition, foxhunting remains the premier sport for English country dwellers, as it has been since the 17th century.

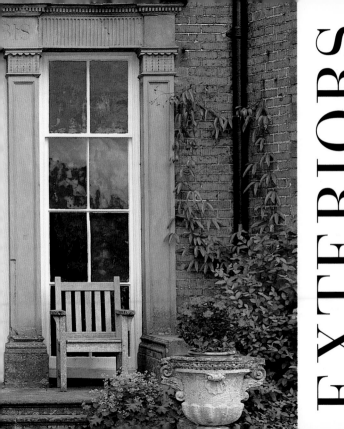

EXTERIORS

ABOVE: *Blo' Norton Hall, an Elizabethan manor house in Norfolk, was built in 1585. Its early form was designed as an E shape, with two gables and decorative step-style brickwork flanking the rectangular hall.* **PRECEDING PAGES:** *Above the doorway of this Georgian home is the name of the wife of one of its earlier owners.*

Below: *Blo' Norton Hall shown from the other side, with the additions of the characteristic half-timbering and high chimneys of the later Elizabethan period. English houses typically were added on to, rather than demolished and rebuilt.*

This wonderfully romantic house in Norfolk, built on the site of a Carmelite priory in 1652, belonged to a local seafaring merchant. The knapped-flint façade (stone broken into small pieces) and redbrick quoins are typical of local East Anglian architecture. The graceful carved stone gables, high chimneys, and intricate brickwork, with a sunken garden beneath, exemplify the English genius for combining common sense with elegance.

34

ABOVE, ABOVE LEFT, AND LEFT:
*English country house façades
reveal their history: 16th-cen-
tury thatch, 17th-century pedi-
mented windows, and a massive Georgian wing show the
range of British architecture
through the ages.* **FAR LEFT:** *An
entrance to a Georgian house
near Wales features magnificent carved wooden gates.*

These fine 18th-century Italian iron gates, set into high stone pillars with plinths, enclose the west garden of Doddington Hall, in Lincolnshire. The allée of clipped yew leads out, in the Elizabethan manner, to the landscape beyond.

40

ABOVE: *To banish doubt, this 17th-century heavy oak door proclaims its date, 1653, with the initials of, probably, the first owner of the house.* **LEFT:** *The English country house as transformed into a doll's house. Sternly classical, it is a Georgian fantasy in miniature, crowned with a family motto in Latin.*

41

ABOVE: *Until recently, the 18th-century stable buildings at Sledmere House were home to one of the most famous studs in the country.*
RIGHT: *The third story of this Jacobean farmhouse was added in the 1780s.*

LEFT: *Riders take their morning exercise past a wing of Heydon Hall, in Norfolk.*

BELOW: *Lived in by the Bulwer family since the 18th century, Heydon Hall is a magnificent example of the Elizabethans' genius.*

ABOVE: *A driveway with high hedges leads to the stables of an estate near the Welsh border that dates from Georgian times.*
RIGHT: *Sledmere House in winter beckons in the snow.*

Nestling under the Downs in Wiltshire, this elegant Georgian house, with horses grazing in the front pasture, was enlarged by its Victorian owners. The front door pediment still shows traces of its 19th-century past.

ABOVE: *A flagstone path leads to the door of the pool pavilion at Biddesden, in Wiltshire.* **RIGHT:** *Biddesden was built in 1711 by General Webb, one of the Duke of Marlborough's colleagues. The tower houses the bell he was awarded for his exploits in battle.*

The magnificent façade of Biddesden shows the art of 18th-century architecture at its most extroverted. The brick- and stonework, well-proportioned windows, and pleasing lines speak as well of General Webb's artistic eye as of his military skills. Its fine state of preservation is due in part to the Guinness family, which has owned the house since 1931.

ABOVE AND ABOVE RIGHT: *At Sledmere, an 18th-century folly (like a film set, the front is a castle, the rear a farm) was built to provide an amusing view from the big house across the field.* **RIGHT:** *A fine thatched barn in Wiltshire.* **FAR RIGHT:** *An example of rustic stonework, very popular in the 18th century.*

Well dressed in old lichen, a boy plays a tune on his pipe, serenading the lawn mower that peeks shyly out of the side doorway of Heydon Hall, a 16th-century manor house.

ABOVE: *Paint and flowers turn a simple back door into a work of art.* **LEFT:** *The 18th-century stables at Biddesden, built out of brick and stone and decorated with paint and flowers, seem too beautiful to be appreciated only by horses.*

ABOVE: *The austere façade of Sledmere House, built in the 18th century, during the "golden age" of English country houses.*
LEFT: *Heale House, a 17th-century manor with exquisite gardens, where King Charles II briefly hid following his defeat by Cromwell at the Battle of Worcester in 1651.*

The Convent in the Woods, in Stourton, Wiltshire, is a small Gothic folly built about 1765 by the landscape architect Sir Henry Hoare, who was an ardent admirer of the rustic and the irregular.

GARDENS

ABOVE: *The gardens at Hergest Croft, in Herefordshire. The designs include Elizabethan-style herb beds, with rosemary, chives, mint, golden marjoram, thyme, rue, and sorrel enclosed within boxwood hedges.* **PRECEDING PAGES:** *A brick path winds through a cozy kitchen garden in East Anglia.*

BELOW: *The Hergest Croft gardens are designed with wide swaths of lawn, perennial borders, and more naturally planted areas, including one of the finest collections of trees and shrubs in the country.*

ABOVE: *Artist James Reeve designed a "folly" for his garden in Somerset—a flower-covered conservatory gateway to nowhere.* **LEFT:** *In Reeve's garden, terra-cotta planters and kitchen chairs share space with rosemary and climbing roses.*

In the garden of a Georgian house, a classical statue is removed from its pedestal and given a new green home in a niche carved out of a yew hedge.

Stourpaine, an unpretentious family house in a Dorset village, has a formal front garden with a croquet lawn defined by a long, low brick wall and decorative urns.

*Geraniums, lobelia, and ivy
spill out of this urn. At right,
a homemade drainpipe adds
an extra touch of color.*

ABOVE: *A stone arch and small pool, designed by Lanning Roper, decorate this garden.* **RIGHT:** *A flower-walk in a Victorian kitchen garden.*

LEFT: *A high brick wall is covered by climbing roses.*
BELOW: *Garden borders with lawn paths and flower beds designed by Lanning Roper.*

Wonderful old steps at Biddesden, mottled with lichen, are enhanced by touches of carefully planted color—dianthus, hebe, campanula, creeping jenny, forget-me-nots, rosemary, lavender, and thyme.

ABOVE: *Old apple trees give shade to a garden path.*
RIGHT: *Untrustworthy topiary buttresses "support" the walls of a garden at Biddesden. Between the buttresses are miniature gardens planted with wisteria, climbing roses, foxglove, and poppies.*

ABOVE: *Roses and lavender crowd the elegant iron gates of the gardens at Helmingham Hall.* **RIGHT:** *Honeysuckle clings to the stone wall of Deene Park in Northamptonshire.*

LEFT AND BELOW: *Details of colorful flower borders seen in English gardens. Many were inspired by Gertrude Jekyll, who believed that a garden should be like a painting.*

ABOVE: *An indoor garden—geraniums, fuchsia, and campanula in a greenhouse at Hergest Croft.* **LEFT:** *Pink roses, purple irises, and red honeysuckle decorate the warm brick around these Georgian bay windows.*

LEFT: *A landscape of lawns and fruit trees.* **BELOW:** *A conservatory window with a family bust brings the garden indoors.* **FAR LEFT:** *Staircase to romance, planted with cotoneaster, moss, and alchemilla.*

ABOVE AND LEFT: *Plants run wild in a garden in Kent, where cupids and urns add architectural interest.*

Looking Inside

THE *interiors of English country houses started to be taken seriously only in the 18th century, when the architect also tended to do the interior decorating. William Kent, the Chippendale family, and Robert Adam, for instance, took an immense interest in the insides of their houses, and the English still treasure their stucco, moldings, and furniture.*

It became fashionable to enhance rooms with not only inherited treasures but also objects found abroad, mostly through imperial travels and astute purchases. You might have wonderful things, however, but you did not flaunt them. A man once admired Lord Derby's Chippendale chairs. Said his lordship, "Damn cheek, that fella noticing my chairs."

While in medieval times the hall was the main living and eating room, dining rooms were important additions when entertaining became a way to show off your status. Dining rooms always had two doors—one for the gentry, one for the servants. With the decline of the servant class and increasing financial problems, the kitchen became a more important room for family and friends to meet. As for the bedroom, Elizabethans invented the four-poster bed for both warmth and privacy. Although the Victorians decided that the hangings promoted airlessness, and were therefore unhygienic, most English country houses still use them.

There have been some well-known English decorators in modern times, but most of the English disavow the idea of a house looking "decorated." For decorative arts devotees, this aversion must be regarded as a limitation. Yet every room pictured here expresses a remarkable individuality. It is on the details that the eye must linger—a wall of pictures, a mantelpiece, a desk—for each tells a story as unique as may be found in any anthology. It is these details that give the rooms their hospitable look and provide the air of relaxed elegance that is the envy of imitators.

PRECEDING SPREAD: *This magnificent hall, used as a family meeting place, has a fine marble floor and an English painted cabinet.*

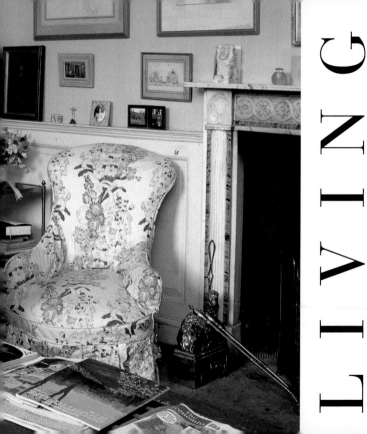

LIVING

RIGHT: *Red-striped wallpaper and red upholstery add warmth to this semi-oval library in Norfolk.* **PRECEDING PAGES:** *An informal sitting room with family pictures and a chintz-covered slipper chair.*

BELOW: *Typically English in its casual look, this flower arrangement contains alchemilla, foxglove, and salvia.*

ABOVE LEFT: *A finely curved staircase in a Norfolk rectory is hung with family portraits.* **ABOVE RIGHT:** *A family portrait at Deene Park, by an unknown artist, is of Sir Robert Salusbury (1756–1817).*

As sunlight streams in, the drawing room of Heydon Hall glows with its red walls (the paint matching an original wallpaper) and the creamy upholstery on the sofa and chair.

ABOVE: *This library, with its round mahogany table, doubles as a study for the owner, a judge. The small walnut desk is piled high with legal briefs.* **LEFT:** *Red silk–covered walls enhance a collection of family portraits.*

The drawing room of Stour-paine in Dorset shows traces of past family travels, with an Indian coverlet on the coffee table, lace, velvet, and patchwork cushions, and an Indian tea caddy as a lamp base. Unmatched cotton slipcovers for the sofa and chairs add coziness.

Originally merchants' samples, these miniature table objects now decorate a Queen Anne–period doll's house (one of the oldest in the world) in Heydon Hall, Norfolk. The candlesticks are Charles II silver.

Miniature pewter and china plates and cups, all to perfect scale, enhance the dresser of this doll's house kitchen. Note the little cheese grater—it could have been made yesterday.

The unexceptional chimney of Wiveton, in East Anglia, has been beautifully stenciled. Family pictures adorn the walls, and plain-colored slipcovers enhance the decorative effect of the wall painting.

ABOVE, ABOVE LEFT, AND LEFT:
*A crowded coffee table, an airy
staircase, and a trompe l'oeil
bookcase (it is in fact a door)
are some details of English
country decorating.* **FAR LEFT:** *A
subtle blue-and-green palette
gives light and air to this room
in Blacklands, Wiltshire. The
Victorian fire screen contains
stuffed birds and butterflies.*

The decoration in Wiveton's drawing room is unnervingly simple—no chintz or other patterns disrupt the harmony of line and color. Bookcases conceal part of the opening, formerly made by double doors, into the billiard room (now the dining room) beyond. To the right of the doorway is a massive 18th-century Italian inlaid cabinet.

The private sitting room of Doddington Hall, in Lincolnshire. Its floor and huge fireplace reveal that it was once part of the original kitchen. The balcony was inspired by a trip to Amsterdam and made by a local carpenter out of one of Doddington's walnut trees.

ABOVE: *The red drawing room at Blacklands has green piping for the slipcovers, a mixture of check patterns, and family pictures.*
RIGHT: *A square red-painted hall in a Georgian house contains inherited portraits, a 19th-century double-sized chair, a mantelpiece decorated with dog-medicine bottles, and sleeping quarters for the dog.*

At Bereleigh, in Hampshire, a particularly fine boot rack displays rubber boots, hunting boots, walking boots, and a rare elaborately carved stand-up boot remover. To the right, a hunting, shooting, fishing, and sun hat collection.

Heydon Hall offers a typical sight in the country: boots, flowers, hunting equipment, boot polish, and family paraphernalia. This would be called a mudroom in America.

ABOVE: *A sign of bygone times at Doddington Hall in Lincoln-shire: a row of early Georgian servants' bells, with the name of each room (where the call originated) inscribed beneath.*
RIGHT: *A corner of the private hall at Doddington Hall. The stenciling in both pictures was done by Felicity Binyon and Elizabeth Macfarlane.*

Bereleigh, a farmhouse in Hampshire, contains this wonderfully busy hall. Dating from 1600, it seems almost medieval in function, serving as both study and sitting room, as well as visitors' center. Hanging by the desk is a collection of horse whips and hunting horns.

This room in what was formerly a barn in Devon has been turned into the warm living room of sculptor Elisabeth Frink. The furniture is pine and mahogany; the sofa is covered in corduroy, the armchair and matching pillow in chintz.

ABOVE: *The upstairs landing of Stourpaine has become a pretty resting place, with a sofa covered in cotton ticking and a chintz slipper (or balloon) blind.* **LEFT:** *This drawing room is decorated with a tapestry hanging behind the Chinese cabinet, silk and linen slipcovers, and Ionic columns replacing a wall.*

ABOVE, ABOVE LEFT, AND LEFT: *Three chintzes from the Colefax & Fowler collection—Bowood (a John Fowler chintz dating from the 1930s), Tree Poppy, and Eugenie.* **FAR LEFT:** *Blue Roses, a fabric design by the late, great Geoffrey Bennison.*

A rare early woodblock-printed wallpaper, dating from 1765—a time when a tax on wallpapers had made them very expensive.

ABOVE LEFT: *A wallpaper frieze dating from 1820, with a striking vine theme in relief.* **ABOVE RIGHT:** *A beautiful Liberty fabric pattern, dating from the 19th century, entitled Melrose.*

ABOVE LEFT: *Another rare Liberty fabric design, called Clandon.*
ABOVE RIGHT: *Wallpaper from a 19th-century woodblock of one of England's most famous designers, William Morris.*

ABOVE: *The faded look of this chintz is intentional. The designer, Geoffrey Bennison, copied old fabrics without trying to brighten them. Bird and Basket came from an old chair cover.* **RIGHT:** *Peacocks and poppies were a popular theme of Arts and Crafts wallpaper designs.*

DINING

ABOVE: *This Wiltshire kitchen has an unusually wide pine table; a dresser stocked with mugs, plates, and tureens; and a vase of fresh-picked flowers. Its warm walls are a subtle shade of orange.*

Piano-playing as well as cooking takes place in this Dorset kitchen, which belongs to author Rachel Billington. Light and airy with huge flagstones, it has ice-blue walls and rush chairs painted bright blue and white.

ABOVE: *A glass chandelier presides over a scrubbed pine table in the kitchen at Blacklands.* **LEFT:** *The kitchen at Heydon Hall was once a study—hence the inset mahogany bookcases (now displaying china), William Morris wallpaper, and Victorian trophies on the wall.*

143

The greenhouse at Wiveton makes a perfect garden room for entertaining: a striped cloth, unmatched wicker chairs, plants all around—summer pleasures when the English weather allows.

The dining room in this manor house—once owned by King George III's dancing master—has red silk walls, family paintings, and an 18th-century piano.

This shooting lunch at Sledmere House was for men only. In country house life, riding, hunting, and shooting were often activities limited to the menfolk.

*Formerly a stable, sculptor Elisabeth Frink's brightly colored
kitchen retains the stable walls at left. A rolling butcher-block
cart serves as a worktable for the cook.*

The kitchen of this Cornish farmhouse has original beams and a slate slab floor. The dresser and cupboards are painted bright green because the owner "got fed up with pine."

The formal dining room at Biddesden frequently seats twenty for dinner. The chair covers, with their classical motif, were specially designed for the room, which also has an unusual 1930s-style rug on the floor.

The dining room at Aske Hall in Yorkshire shows English living at its simplest. The elegant 18th-century mahogany chairs and finely carved mantelpiece reveal its aristocratic provenance.

Stencil artist Mary Mac-Carthy's classic country kitchen, with its Indian cotton cloth and unmatched cushions on the chairs. Her stenciling decorates the dresser doors.

ABOVE: *A collection of English bone china in coral-painted display niches enhances the eating area of the drawing room at Biddesden.* **RIGHT:** *Glowing apricot walls, a blue embroidered cloth from Damascus, a large gilt mirror, and gilt candelabra make the dining room at Stourpaine sing.*

Known as "the English fridge," larders are often used in country houses to store food. They have small windows to discourage flies and maintain a cool temperature.

This larder in Norfolk is stacked with supplies that require a cool but not frigid climate. (English summers are never very hot.) The left wall is decorated with Mary MacCarthy's wall paintings.

Above: *An unusual country breakfast—a plate of gulls' eggs.* **Left:** *This kitchen, like many English country house kitchens, is big enough to accommodate large numbers, with three separate work spaces.*

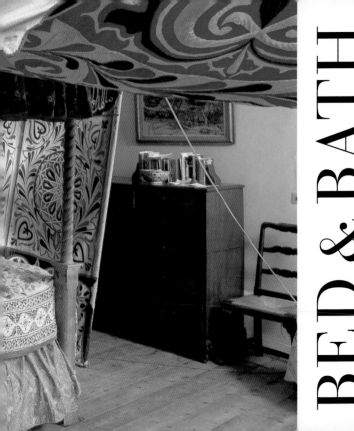

BED & BATH

RIGHT: *An Italian 18th-century gilt headboard dominates this master bedroom, with the plain pine chest and rush matting for contrast.* **PRECEDING PAGES:** *The quilted Durbar tent in a bedroom at Wireton once belonged to a friend of Edward VII.*

This bedroom is French in flavor, with a French four-poster bed decorated with a rare old chintz, and French blue curtains. The Regency drop-leaf table serves as a writing desk for guests.

A Georgian mahogany book-case set into the wall of this bedroom at Heydon Hall reminds guests that the room was once part of a huge upstairs library. The bedstead is brass.

This master bedroom is decorated with pale yellow walls and honeysuckle chintz. The bed hangings are lined with pink-and-white checked cotton, and the bedposts are wrapped in padded chintz.

A flower theme dominates this child's bedroom, with a canopied bed, tablecloths, and armchair all covered in violet chintz. A ceiling frieze and unusual wall hanging add interest.

In this guest bedroom at
Doddington, the walls are
covered in an original
William Morris willow pattern. The blue-and-white
chintz bed hangings are
copied from a French toile.

A simple bedroom in Norfolk is filled with light, enhancing the delicate mauve wallpaper and violet-patterned pillow. Family photographs and portraits are hung on the wall in a very personal way.

Warm colors, a fragile chintz, a comfortable chaise for the dog, and a substantial four-poster bed make for agreeable contrasts in this bedroom at Aske Hall, Yorkshire.

Like the French inlaid wood dressing table, the posts of this bed are intricately decorated. The simple eiderdown and plain bed linens lighten the grandeur of this bedroom in Staffordshire.

ABOVE AND LEFT: *These bedrooms, enhanced with old chintz, Indian cotton, Majorcan ikat fabric, and printed cotton, show the range and variety of fabrics used in English country decorating.*

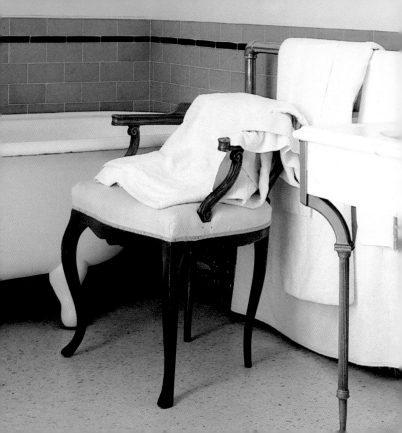

LEFT: *An austere 19th-century men's room, with a marble basin, baroque faucets, a heated towel rail, and a mahogany chair.*
PRECEDING PAGES: *An oasis of comfort at Sledmere House, created by the wallpaper-wrapped bath, sheepskin rug, and gentle colors.*

ABOVE: *A rarity today, a chaise percée (toilet) in stylish English wicker.* **RIGHT:** *The handsome master bath at Blacklands is masculine in feel with brown print wallpaper, paneled bath and basin, and mahogany wardrobe.*

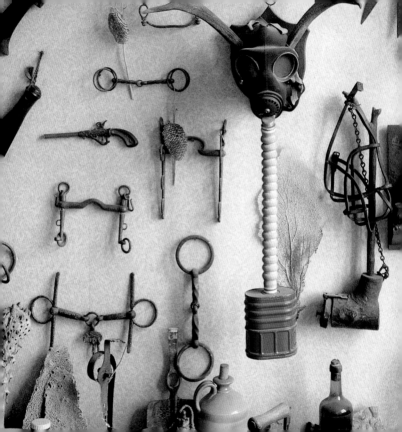

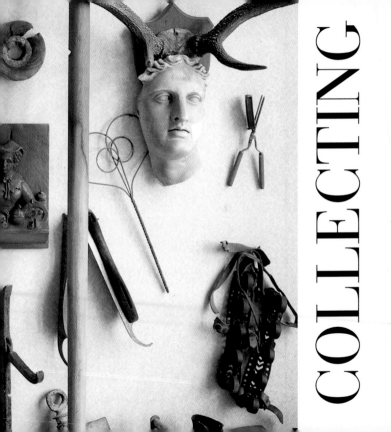

COLLECTING

*Mason's Ironstone was one of
the many Staffordshire potter-
ies producing useful dishes
that also look handsome when
arrayed on a kitchen dresser.*
PRECEDING PAGES: *An eccentric
mix found in an attic.*

ABOVE: *A group of Stafford-shire dogs surround a china model of Garibaldi.* **LEFT:** *This china hat, decorated with fresh flowers, is one of several collected from antiques shops around the country.*

ABOVE AND FAR RIGHT: *Shelves of Staffordshire jugs, cache-pots, tankards, vases, and a famous cow pitcher advertising "pure milk."* **RIGHT:** *Popular Staffordshire copper luster dogs.*

PURE MILK

MILK·SOLD·HERE

ABOVE: *A Mason's Ironstone meat dish.* **RIGHT:** *A collection of blue-and-white Sledmere china hung on a wall in the dining room at Sledmere House.*

ABOVE: *As well as jugs with historical references painted on them (these dating from 1879 to 1883), Staffordshire turned out many animal designs, such as this brown-and-yellow Trojan lion.* **LEFT:** *A fine family collection of blue-and-white Chinese export porcelain.*

The attic corridor at Doddington Hall contains an invaluable storehouse of paintings and discarded heirlooms, as well as the "antler wall," designed to scare small children and impress the grown-ups.

Collections of early English children's books reveal masterly art-
work, such as this title page of Us, An Old-Fashioned Story, by
the beloved Victorian author Mrs. Molesworth, designed most
elegantly by Walter Crane and dated 1923.

Every English child knew this book, A Child's Garden of Verses, *by Robert Louis Stevenson, but only the lucky ones would own this beautiful version, decorated on the title page with a watercolor by A. H. Watson.*

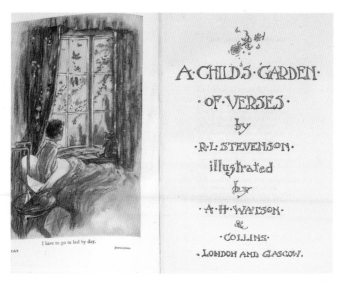

I have to go to bed by day.

frontispiece

A·CHILD'S·GARDEN·
·OF·VERSES·
by
·R·L·STEVENSON·
illustrated
by
·A·H·WATSON·
&
·COLLINS·
·LONDON AND GLASGOW.